Edward Cowell Brice

The Prison at Philippi

And Other Sacred Poems

Edward Cowell Brice

The Prison at Philippi
And Other Sacred Poems

ISBN/EAN: 9783744753326

Printed in Europe, USA, Canada, Australia, Japan

Cover: Foto ©Thomas Meinert / pixelio.de

More available books at **www.hansebooks.com**

PRISON AT PHILIPPI

AND OTHER

SACRED POEMS

BY

REV. EDWARD COWELL BRICE, B.A.,
VICAR OF NEWNHAM, GLOUCESTERSHIRE.

London:
LONGMAN'S, GREEN, READER, AND DYER.

Gloucester:
EDMUND NEST, 155, WESTGATE STREET.

1876.

CONTENTS.

	PAGE
THE PRISON AT PHILIPPI	3
CHRISTMAS DAY	10
NAZARETH	22
HOLY LAND—SKETCHES AND THOUGHTS	37
ZACCHEUS AND BARTIMEUS	52
BETHANY	58
EASTER DAY	64
ASCENSION DAY	74
THE FIRST RESURRECTION	77
MIDNIGHT TRAVELS	80
CHRISTMAS 1875	84
THE WELL AT BETHLEHEM	88
HOW SHALL I BE SATISFIED?	91
"VERILY I SAY"	94
STANDING AND KNOCKING	97
HARVEST HOME	101
DAVID'S HARP	104
FROM THE GERMAN	106
YOUNG EDWARD'S GRAVE	107
A MEDITATION	110
THE OCTOGENARIAN	112

ERRATA.

In page 28, line 7, for recent, read *centre;* in page 66, line 2, for it were told itself, read *itself we're told.*

POEMS

BY

REV. EDWARD COWELL BRICE, B.A.

THE PRISON AT PHILIPPI.

"At midnight Paul and Silas *prayed and sang praises unto God*, and *the prisoners heard them*."—Acts 16, 25.

'TIS midnight round Philippi's walls,
    And grandeur's echoes cease to swell;
The lyre is hush'd amid the halls,
    The trumpet in the citadel.
'Tis darkness through the mystic grove,
    The column'd courts, the marble ways;
No votary sues Olympic Jove,
    And silent is Minerva's praise;

The worship of Apollo's ray
Went with the last bright hours of day;
    The adoring crowd,
    The pæans loud,
The rich, the garlanded, the proud
    Have pass'd away.

But ah! where deep the dungeon lies
    Within that lordly city's bounds,
There doth the voice of prayer arise,
    And there the saintly hymn resounds.
Hark! to the True, Eternal Lord
    Two holy prisoners wake and cry;
To Him they sing with sweet accord,
    And heavenward look with faithful eye.
To Christ they sing, to Christ they pray,
To Him the only God of Day,
    Of Wisdom, Might;
For His dear sake they wear the chain,
Take the stern lash, endure the pain,
And now His brightest smiles they gain
    At dead of night.

Messiah's wondrous love they sing,
  Who left his star-encircled throne
Peace on his gracious lips to bring,
  And make their rebel hearts His own.
They utter forth His balmy name
  Amidst the dungeon's poisonous air,
And bless their Lord for all the shame
  That he hath deemed them fit to bear.
Ah! blind Philippi little knows
How beautiful the steps of those
Whom Jesus sends!—her bonds compel
To the vile prison's inmost cell
    Their pilgrim feet;
But though the iron clogs the limb,
The faith-wing'd spirit breathes with Him
    In union sweet.
Hark! the hosannas louder swell,
Still on Immanuel's name they dwell
    With hallow'd glee;
His was the arm that fought so well,
Broke the worst bonds of sin and hell,
    And set them free.

THE PRISON AT PHILIPPI.

Through the long low arches going
   Spreads the unaccustom'd sound,
Undefiled, and sweetly flowing
   Into every ward around.
Where the murmurs of affliction,
   Or dread curses lately fell,
With the feverish malediction
   Of the care-worn sentinel;
Where the robber clank'd his chain
Beseeching Mercury in vain;
Where to fabled Mars for aid
Fiercely the bondaged warrior prayed;
And the assassin chafed his mood
In His own den of solitude—
Echoes there the hymn of peace
To the God who can release.

   Through the grated opening small
   Of each cell, the accents fall,
   Rousing every sullen head
   From its straw or sackcloth bed.

THE PRISON AT PHILIPPI.

   See, the temple-plunderer waking
   Listens with astounded ear,
   Though the strain be gentle quaking
   Lest the deity be near.
So sacredly those numbers roll
They are a terror to his soul.
With frozen heart and dull despair
Down he sinks upon his lair.
Awakens too the bandit bold
   Who late from Macedonia's hills
Was wont to ravage dale and wold
   Till now a gloomy nook he fills.
Scarce out of sleep, the echoes seem
The music of a mountain dream,
Or some unearthly warbled lore
' Mid the wild groves of sycamore.
He starts, feels the cold ponderous chain,
Then reckless turns to sleep again.

   Hark! hark! 'tis an earthquake's roar!
      Bursts the dread thunder

The deep vaults under,
Rending the prison's solid floor—
Wide fly the folds of every door—
From every hand in every cell
Drop the bolt and manacle.
The Angel of the King of Saints
   Stoops upon his secret wings!
Marble crumbles, iron faints,
   Brass from its hold of vigour springs
     Before his way!
     Wild with dismay
The jailor out of slumber starting,
Along the shivering pavement darting,
Sees the chambers opening all,
Sees the prisoners free from thrall,
And with desperation fierce
Draws the sword his breast to pierce;
But instantly the shout of Paul,
" Do thyself no harm, for all
Are here within the prison's wall,"
Arrests his hand—forward he springs,
Sinks down before the saints, and clings

THE PRISON AT PHILIPPI.

Round the blest feet he dared to bind—
"Servants of God!" is all his cry,
"Oh how shall such a wretch as I
    Salvation find"?—
"Believe in Jesus, all Divine,
And salvation shall be thine."

They speak to him the heavenly Word,
The gracious message of the Lord,
To him and all his house.—That hour,
That self-same hour, at first so dread
With the rending earthquake's power,
With the mighty Angel's tread—
He took them from the vault profound
Where he had thrust them, bleeding, bound,
And "wash'd their stripes"—then (no delay)
Baptized, his sins were wash'd away,
With Jesu's cleansing blood his stay.
Those holy ones he brought above
    To chambers of his own abode,
"Set meat before them"—served with love—
    Rejoiced in Christ—believed in God.

CHRISTMAS DAY

Luke 2, 1—20.

AUGUSTUS issued a decree
    That "all the world should taxēd be"—
The orb of Roman sovereignty.
What was by tyranny projected,
Was by the God of heaven directed
To bring to pass in place and time
A prophesied event, the prime,
That Christ of royal David's stem,
Was to "come forth" at Bethlehem.
For by imperial commands
The populations of the lands
Must all to their own cities come,

Taxes to pay to mighty Rome.
So Joseph and his sacred spouse,
"Of David's lineage and house,"
Compelled by Cæsar's edict, came
From Nazareth to Bethlehem;
And in brief time, the journey done,
Mary "brought forth her first born Son."

But in this narrative we find
An incident which seems designed,
Deeply to interest the mind.
Joseph and Mary, holy pair,
Met with no welcome greeting there,
"No room" remained in Bethlehem's inn,
When they applied amid the din
Made by the crowd their ends to win;
Nought but a cold and stubborn "Nay"
Came from that caravanserai.
O'er-wearied and in deepest need—
In *her* case it was deep indeed—
They were at once obliged to crave

The shelter of a peasant's cave
Amongst his cattle—To this day
A spot where pilgrims flock to pray—
And there was Jesus, "David's Son"
And "David's Lord," the twain in one,
Born to their solace—also there
The cattle's rustic crib to share.

In clothes that Hebrew infants wore,
Prepared with earnest care before
At Nazareth, by her no doubt,
Ere they commenced their anxious route—
She swathed Him with the tenderest skill,
To guard Him in such place from ill,
And when not treasured in her breast,
The manger was his needful rest.
This was the scene—this lowly shed
Gave Him this humble infant bed.
The thought o'erwhelms the mind, that He,
Th' Incarnate Lord of All, should be
Thus domicil'd, His place of birth

The very rudest on the earth.
But in all this devoutly see
His infinite humility,
His love which emptied self of glory,
And made a sorrowed life His story,
That his true followers might rise
To mansions in his own bright skies.

But oh! how mournful to reflect
What multitudes this Lord reject,
And from their hearts His truth exclude,
And e'en the thought of Him extrude.
Man's heart is like, 'tis sad to say,
A certain caravanserai.
There the whole world may entrance find,
And worldly things of every kind.
Does Folly knock?   It is let in.
Does Pleasure?   It is sure to win.
In special instances the door
Opens more widely than before.
Does Money show an entrance fee?

None is more welcome instantly.
Does Business ask? What numbers still
Seem to be crowding in until
Every chamber they must fill.
Does Care before the portal stand?
The heart admits the sad demand.
Do even Sorrow, Grief, and Woe,
Press strangely to come in? 'Tis so.
There's "room" for all excepting One,
And that is Jesus, God's dear Son.

Yet what blest hopes His grace affords!
What are His own most precious words?
"Lo! I stand at the door and knock:"
If any man the door unlock,
If any man will hear my voice,
And open it, I will rejoice,
And will come in and sup, and he
Shall hold communion with me.
Oh! happy they who hear that voice,
And make that happiness their choice;

CHRISTMAS DAY.

Who yield a heart grown hard in sin,
For peace and purity within !

The cave of the Nativity,
And three-fold Holy Family,
We left awhile—to introduce
Some thoughts which haply may have use
If the analogy between
Man's heart and Bethlehem's inn be seen ;
But to return,—At early morn
First from the time the Babe was born,
Arrived in haste a pious band
Of Shepherds from the hills at hand,
And the night sheep-folds old in fame
From David's loved and honoured name.

Angelic teachings led them here—
The true signs given them all appear—
They gaze with reverent awe around—
Those for whom they searched are found.

THE LEADING SHEPHERD SPEAKS.

Blessed Mother, to Thee all joy!
We hail the new-born Heavenly Boy!
The angel of the Lord this night,
Arrayed in garb of glorious light,
Came while we watched beside the fold
And tidings of great wonder told.
He bade us hasten on our way
To see the Saviour born this day
In David's city, and we're come
To view Him in His humble home.
With love and joy our hearts receive Him,
We see, we wonder, we believe Him,
We bow with reverence before Him,
We humbly worship and adore Him.
We own him David's Son and Heir,
Our Shepherd King who led with care
His flocks in fields the very same
As those to which God's angel came
To us poor Shepherds—how can we

CHRISTMAS DAY.

Describe his mien and majesty?
The Lords own glory shone around,
We trembled on the hallowed ground.
"Fear not," the angel said, and then
Telling us of great joy to men,
Suddenly from above the sky,
E'en from the throne of God most high,
Filling the brightened realm of air,
Appearing with the angel there,
Thousands upon thousands came
Of God's immediate host to claim
The joy of praising His great name.
They were above, around, before us,
And we all heard their lofty chorus.
"Glory to God" they nobly sang,
Their music through our bosoms rang;
"Glory to God" shall ever be
The outburst of our psalmody.

The shepherds left to spread abroad
The tidings sent them by their God;

And praising Him for all they'd seen
According as the signs had been;
Still singing, "Glory" ever be
   The burden of our psalmody.
We too should be prompt to raise
Glory to God in loftiest praise,
To Him in "highest" heavens above,
And for His abounding love
To all "on earth" whose hearts record
"A Saviour which is Christ the Lord."

Mary, pattern for pious thought,
Pondered on all her God had wrought.
The things she heard, and saw, and knew,
In sacredness profoundly grew;
Too deep to others to impart,
She kept them in her own deep heart.
And we, in honouring Christmas Day
With all the happiness we may,
And while festivity it brings,
Should also ponder on these things.

CAROL.

COLD are the nights in dark December,
    Wintry blasts are frequent then;
But ever *One* night we remember,
    Blessed above all to men.

'Tis that when Christ expected long
    Was born of woman, God's own Son,
And heaven proclaimed in rapt'rous song
    That endless blessings had begun.

Bethlehem's hill-side fields were lying
    Darkly in the dead of night;
Shepherds their faithful labours plying
    Dimly by the watch-fire's light;

When suddenly night turned to day,
    Day brighter than before was known;
From heaven to earth was one bright ray,—
    The Lord's great angel had come down!

Oh! what transcendent news he brought us!
    Birth of Jesus, Babe Divine!
What lessons of God's love he taught us,
    In tidings of His great design!

Jesus, Saviour, Lord, and Shepherd,
    Born to save from sin and woe;
To guard His flock from wolf and leopard,
    And defend from every foe.

Our hearts then prize cold dark December,
    Its Christmas night must make it dear;
And with our lov'd ones we'll remember
    With joy its blessings and its cheer.

CHRISTMAS DAY.

* * * * * *

Deem not the humble carols lost
    At midnight sung, or early morn,
Oft in keen air and nipping frost,
    To hail in heart the Saviour born.

To some, we trust, warm slumber taking,
    The while beneath their window frame
The strain is heard, 'tis sweet on waking
    To list to His ascending name.

NAZARETH.

Luke 2, 42—52.

"JESUS of Nazareth"—a name
 Humblest of all, yet great in fame
And precious, other names above,
To hearts of humble faith and love.
'Twas there within a circling belt
Of quiet little hills He dwelt
With His blest mother thirty years,
Working with Joseph, it appears,
As carpenter, a good vocation,
Almost a sacred occupation,
As needs we deem it now since He
Employed His sacred hands to be
Helps to parental cares, and prove
Submissiveness of filial love

NAZARETH.

Amid that sweet, secluded vale
His years were but the briefest tale;
With piety the same in all,
Mark'd days 'twere needless to recall.
Yet one great incident occurred,
When twelve years old, which deeply stirred
The parents' bosom, when with them
He went up to Jerusalem
To keep the Passover, and when
The company set forth again,
Unknown to them he stayed behind,
Impelled by secret force of mind,
Sought for three days, and none could find,
Oh! what perplexing, anxious fears
Had Mary in the midst of tears.
At length they spied the wondrous Child
Calm, self-possessed, as ever mild,
With doctors in the temple sitting,
Hearing, and asking questions fitting.
His mother chided—but said He,
" How is it that ye sought for me?

Wist ye not I must be about
My Father's business?"—Here came out
That He was God's incarnate Son,
And to perceive had uow begun,
What had not reached His mother's mind,
His Heavenly Father's work assigned.

It may be, to His youthful soul
This was the opening of the whole—
Of wisdom ever freshly learned,
And verities still more discerned.
And this for many years to come
At Nazareth His humble home,
Till His great mission called Him thence,
Prepared all blessings to dispense,
To teach, to heal, to save the world,
With Satan's empire downward hurled.
Meanwhile Himself He meekly bore
Towards earthly lov'd ones as before,
"Subject unto them"—subject too
To Him in love profound He knew,

His Father in eternal union,
Ever with Him in communion;
And often to converse in prayer
And lofty meditation there,
He climbed, no doubt, in early day
The highest hills that round Him lay,
Their smooth and turfy tops attaining,
And views of wondrous beauty gaining—
Tabor entitled to "rejoice"
In sacred fame's perpetual voice,
And mountain ranges which supply
Deep interest to the raptured eye.
Down to the left the sight could gain
Esdraelon's immemorial plain;
And straight before Him Carmel rose,
Signal for judgment on God's foes;
Associate with Elijah's name,
Jehovah's honour, Baal's shame.
Beyond, the "Great Sea" stretched its bar,
Washing unseen the isles afar;
With Carmel jutting on the coast,

NAZARETH.

Old Tyre and Sidon once its boast.
Cool airs came over to the hills
When Jesus gazed—a breeze that fills
With soft delight—coming to meet Him,
And with refreshing power to greet Him.
And who shall say that while that breeze
And all around was felt to please,
The thought, my Father made them all,
Would not mysteriously call
Another and companion thought,
That " Without Him was not aught
Of anything that e'er was wrought?"*

We leave the hill-tops now to view
   The dear Redeemer in the vale,
Walking where'er the sweet flowers grew,
   The chief of which He loved to hail.

* John i. 3.

This was the Huley Lily, which,
In beauty and adornment rich,
Abounds in northern Galilee.
The traveller delights to see,
While about Tabor's base he roves,
Their clusters in the old oak groves;
And in the valleys all around
And bosky uplands they are found,
Mostly amid strong thorns which make
It difficult the plant to take—
Nature's tribute of protection
To what is exquisite perfection.
One traveller dilates so well
On what his memory loves to dwell,
I would that my poor verse had power
To paint the incomparable flower,
Which he declares where'er it blows
Transcends in beauty Sharon's rose.
It is very large and tall,
Distinct in character from all
The lilies of our cooler zone,

Though these have merits of their own.
Its blossoms in compartments such,
So perfect, guard from thoughtless touch,
Lest discomposure there should be,
Or tarnished matchless brilliancy,
Or velvet vest with injury.
Three petals from the recent spring
To meet above it towering,
And form a gorgeous canopy,
With which no art could ever vie,
Nor monarch for a throne supply.
These flowers to Jesus so well known
Were at Nazareth as His own,
Remarking them through all His youth,
Selecting them to teach the truth
Of our Heavenly Father's care
Which all may trust and all may share.
"Consider how the lilies grow,
They toil not, spin not," and yet know
That even Israel's greatest king
With all the wealth that power could bring,

And all the splendour pride to please,
"Was not arrayed like one of these."

To the Sacred Song of Songs
Praise of these lilies oft belongs;
And it is curious how they keep
A singular companionship.
Where'er they group in vales and dells
There congregate the fond Gazelles.
Herds of this loveliest tribe of deer
Affect to feed with lilies near.
Roaming beneath old Tabor's height
You scare them from their chief delight.

It would indeed be sweet to find
In this old city what the mind
Could dwell upon with veneration
If known as truthful in relation
To Jesus, but saving one spot,
Which we will notice, there is not
Of all that is pretended aught

Which is not with deception fraught.
Ignorance and fraud begin,
Superstition confirms the sin.
They show you here at Nazareth
(The mention of it stops one's breath)
"Joseph's work-shop"—sure that there
Jesus once wrought as carpenter;
"Mary's kitchen," "Mary's cave,"
The spot where Gabriel stood and gave
To her the great "Annunciation;"
The mount called of "Precipitation,"
Far from the town its present station;
The Synagogue where Jesus took
And quoted from the Holy Book;
Added another monstrous fable,
The "veritable dining-table"
Of Christ and his Apostles, when
The last had not been chosen then.
These falsities, alas! needs must
Create contempt and move disgust
In minds of truth and piety;

Grief, too, that sacred things should be
Subject to seeming mockery.
Besides, they are not only lies,
But gross impossibilities;
The crumbling nature of the stone
Of the whole district does alone
Make certain there's no building, wall,
Or fragment, howsoever small,
Of ancient Nazareth but must
Ages ago have gone to dust.

I freely own that not a few
Of these particulars I drew
From the work, "The Land and the Book;"
And though a liberty I took,
It will be well if you, my friend,
Will do just what I recommend,—
Go to a convenient stall,
Buy the Book, and read it All.

But while such falsities abound,
Happily there is one spot found
Truthful, delightful to the mind
From the sweet thoughts with it combined.
It is the fine old massive well
Of which all travellers love to tell,
And in perfection still remains,
The only one the town contains,
Or ever did; besides this one
Ancient Nazareth had none.
Here to this day the Nazarenes,
Where from the sun soft foliage screens,
Crowd round the margin to obtain,
With vessels numberless to drain
The precious product, for elsewhere
All water is extremely rare.

And here did Jesus, beyond doubt,
All misgivings, too, without,
Come often for the needful store
Full eighteen hundred years and more

NAZARETH.

Now past, each time with loving care,
And courtesy to others there,
To fill His mother's pitcher,—then
Bearing it to her hands again.

Does the remoteness of an act
Destroy the truthfulness of fact?
We may not, must not, cannot doubt,
Nor are we left a proof without;
We know what *He* was sure to do,
And he did it because *True.*

Ah! should you e'er by that well's brink
A traveller stand, and deeply think
That He, although so long ago,
Placed His blest feet so nearly so,
'Twill be a thought to bear afar,
And please the mind where'er you are.
But yet still more let memory dwell
On timely words which from Him fell—

" *This* water to quench thirst is vain,
" Whoso drinks will thirst again ;
" But the water which I shall give
" Shall cause him evermore to live ;
" It shall prove a *well* to be
" Springing up everlastingly."

But now we come to that fixed time
When having reached His manhood's prime,
He leaves His mother and His home,
No more 'mid peaceful scenes to roam ;
Or to explore the vales and dells,
Pleased with the lilies and gazelles,
Which objects of the simple kind
Were suited to his gentle mind.
Nor too much now must he devote
E'en to His mother loving thought ;
But His heavenly Father's call
Was to be paramount to all ;
And He set forth at once to be
The Teacher of all Galilee ;

Through towns and villages to go,
Healing all sickness, soothing woe;
Where'er He went all good t'impart—
This His mission which filled His heart.
But when the Passover drew nigh,—
The last to Him, with certainty—
To Judah's capital He bent
His footsteps—His whole soul intent.
There rejected, set at nought,
Before chief priests and rulers brought,
Mocked and scourged, betrayed, denied,
And after these things, crucified.
Suffering thus for you and me,
And sinners all who seek to flee
From sin's desert and misery.
Always, from first to last, His name,
"Jesus of Nazareth," the same.
When upon the Cross suspended,
The while Atonement's work was ended,
His mother and the favourite John,
Broken-hearted, yet gazing on,

Were close beneath Him, and He cried—
"Behold thy Mother!"—deeds replied—
And John so near it saw and read
The Title written o'er His head,
And in his gospel did record
"Jesus of Nazareth"—each word.

HOLY LAND.

SKETCHES AND THOUGHTS.

TO hearts that love the Holy Land
    To do so is a sweet demand,
So strong, so touching is the claim.
There Jesus walked with love; His name
O'erspreads it with a Holy fame.
Infant in arms at Bethlehem,—
Years past, he walked Jerusalem.
Though indignation doomed that city,
His eye beheld with tender pity.
Though their proud hearts were from Him kept,
Over their miseries He wept.
If they had learnt in that their day,

That last which then they threw away,
Things so concerning them to know,
He would have saved them from their woe,
Have gathered them with power beneath
His sheltering arms from danger—death—
E'en as the brooding bird has got
Her fearfully endangered lot
Of little ones in safety's spot
Beneath her wings—but they would not.
Jerusalem was overthrown,
Left scarcely with a stone on stone.
Within its foe-beleaguered walls—
A fact which still the world appals—
A million perished—Woe-struck nation
That scorned to own its visitation!
And 'tis a melancholy thought
How fearful was the ruin brought,
And justly, on those little cities
Ungrateful (so that no one pities)
Which Jesus filled with proofs of power,
And deeds of love from hour to hour.

"Woe unto thee, Chorazin ! Woe
Unto thee, Bethsaida !" for know
That if the mighty works you've seen
In Sidon and in Tyre had been
Wrought for their warning, long ago
They would have sat in sackcloth low.
" And thou, Capernaum, so high
Exalted," 'tis thy doom to lie
In heaps confused and downward thrust
Into dilapidation's dust.

Long did it distress the mind
No traces of the *site* to find ;
For though its melancholy fate
Followed an unrepentant state,
The Lord had sojourned there so long,
His fame for marvels was so strong,
And he had made it central ground
For light and life to radiate round—
That it might be thought tradition
Would have kept up the true position,

And men from time to time would come
And cry, "Here stood Capernaum!"
But no—except perhaps a few
Vague guesses, none cared and none knew.
But happily those days are past,
The sacred site is found at last.
I'm glad the certainty has come.
Long lost to knowledge, guessed by some,
'Tis now discovered at Tell Hum,
Hard by, as it was sure to be,
The well known Lake of Galilee.

IN GALILEE.

"Went about doing good" should be
Deemed, as it were, a diary,
A page of a whole history.
Every where through Galilee,
In country, villages, towns, came
The deaf, the dumb, the palsied, lame,

Possessed with devils, leprous, blind,
Perfect cure at once to find,
Mercy and miracle combined.
Not one did ever on Him call
For help in vain—He healed them all.
Merciful Lord! on Thee *we* call,
Cure the sin-sickness of us all!

NEAR BETHSAIDA.

Multitudes followed where he went,
Till with fatigue and hunger spent
They almost fainted on the way—
He fed them all without delay,
Disposed in ranks by hundreds and
By fifties at His blest command
On a wide district of "green grass; *"
And so the marvel came to pass,
Five loaves and two small fishes were

* Mark vi. 39, 40.

Note.—This is one of many remarkable instances of Mark, under the supposed dictation of Peter, giving more exact particulars than the other Evangelists.

More than enough for thousands there.
Think of the stupendous deed!
Men, women, little ones to feed
Abundantly in hunger's need
From seemingly most scant provision
Requiring infinite division—
Men five thousand, perhaps of others
As many children with their mothers.
All are equally supplied,
And all are fully satisfied.
Marvel on marvel, still to spare
Twelve baskets full besides are there
Of fragments gathered up with care,
Which office the disciples share
By order of the gracious Host,
His goodness bearing all the cost,
"That nothing" of the whole "be lost."
Oh! wonderful and gracious Lord,
The bread from Heaven, the Living Word!
Feed our *souls* in mighty deed,
We are ourselves in greater need.

AT NAIN—A FUNERAL.

The Lord approached the city's gate,
Which he had entered oft of late,
And thence a bier and funeral band
Were passing to a grave at hand.

The dead must have been much beloved,
As crowding sympathizers proved;
It was a youthful corpse, and so
He could have known but little woe.

And yet he had a father lost,
Death had before the threshold crost;
And now the widow, broken-hearted,
Mourned for a dear Child departed.

And ah! there was a deeper grief—
Anguish that seemed beyond relief—
Not alone a widow's son,
He was, alas! her Only One.

HOLY LAND.

Who but He that met the train
Of mourners at the gate of Nain
Effectual comfort could impart
To soothe so desolate a heart?

But Jesus could—His words, "weep not,"
Saved her from sinking on the spot;
She might have met before that hour
Him so renowned for grace and power;

And possibly a slender ray
Of hope into her bosom may
Have darted, that His words implied
He had already death defied.

And now the Lord at once draws near,
And touches with command the bier—
The bearers standing still, He cries,
"Young man, I say to thee, arise!"

HOLY LAND.

"He that was dead sat up and spoke;"
And while the crowd astonished broke
The deep silence, solemnly raising
A shout to Heaven for mercy praising,

Jesus with the tenderest feeling,
His look and voice His heart revealing,
Left not the office to another—
"*He* delivered him to his mother."

AT NAIN—A PENITENT

A pharisee desired the Lord
To honour him with His accord
To eat meat with Him; others were
Invited guests the meal to share.

And when the company were met,
And in their mode at table set,
One *un*invited entered there
With quiet step and mournful air,

And straightway passing came behind
The couch on which the Lord reclined,
And poured her tears upon His Feet,
(The act she felt for *her* most meet.)

And with reverential care
Wiped them with her flowing hair,
Where once the ornamental shone,
But then disgustful, it was gone;

And kissed His feet, devoutly kneeling,
All-unworthy deeply feeling,
Still trembling lest to take that honour
Presumption should be charged upon her;

And drawing forth a box she'd brought
Of spikenard full, so prized and sought,
She broke it, and o'erspread the feet
With an anointing passing sweet.

A single word she did not speak,
Aught to explain she did not seek;
Sure that He knew her deep distress,
Her utter broken-heartedness.

"Her many sins are all forgiven"—
Words of the very God of heaven!—
From sins and sorrows full release—
"Thy faith hath saved thee, go in peace."

ON THE SHORE OF GENNESARET AFTER THE RESURRECTION.

One day at early morning light
Scarcely cleared off from shadowy night,
A Stranger stood beside the Lake
Seeming an interest to take
In certain boats containing seven
Disciples of the Lord from heaven
Returning wearied to the shore,
Their unsuccessful labours o'er.

The Stranger, with kind words to greet,
Cried, "Children, have ye any meat"?
The query a reply soon taught—
They'd toiled all night and nothing caught.
"Cast your net on the ship's right side;"
Useless they thought it, but complied;
When lo! suddenly 'twas full
And hardly possible to pull—
One hundred, fifty-three, great fishes,
Rich amends for late futile wishes;
And, though so over-weighted, yet
There was no rupture of the net.
John perceived at once—a quick word
Whispering to Simon—"'tis the Lord"!
Simon got on his fisher's coat,
Leap'd at once from out the boat,
And push'd to where the Lord was standing,
The rest dragging the net to landing.
Then a miracle to prepare—
A ready fire of coals was there,
And laid thereon were fish and bread.

With voice of sweetness Jesus said,
"Come and dine"—no word was spoken;
Awe-struck, silence was not broken.
Blessing the fishes and the bread,
Jesus at once distributed.
Afterwards turning He addressed
To Peter words his bosom prest.
"Simon, lovest thou Me more
Than these do," or aught worldly store?
"Yea, Lord, Thou knowest that I love
Thee" before all and aught above.
A second time the question came,
And Simon's answer was the same.
A third time—ah! poor Peter grieved,—
How could his bosom be relieved?
It was a deeply painful trial,
He felt it touch his third denial.
But he appealed to Him who knew
All things, all hearts, that *his* was true.
Third time—" Feed my lambs, feed my sheep."
Nor would He now from Peter keep
The solemn future which would be,
When an old man, no longer free,

He should stretch forth his helpless hands,
Begirt and bound with fatal bands,
And follow Him and nobly prove
By the same death his truth and love.
Peter mused deeply—seeing John,
The lov'd disciple, thereupon
He put a question to the Lord
Which seems some insight to afford
To mingled thoughts that stirred his mind
For which he would solution find.
Would John the lov'd one have to die
For Him they both loved equally?
It was presuming, curious too—
"Lord, and what shall this man do?"
Jesus check'd—"What is that to thee?"
My words are, "Follow *thou* Me."
Spoken on Gennesaret's strand;
For the Lord had given command
To meet once more in Galilee,
Promising there Himself to be
After his rising from the dead,
Their living Lord, their glorious Head.

The noted words, so strong which He
To Peter said, let the same be
Of interest deep to you and me;
And in picturing the scene
Where they were spoken first, I ween
They sound with sweetness all the more
As echoed from Gennesaret's shore.

Forget not—Christ would have us see
In sound religion there must be
INDIVIDUALITY.
Peter was to follow on
Irrespectively of John.
And oh! the motive and the power
At every step, in every hour!
"Lovest thou me"?
"Follow thou me."
Sequence how close!—the faithful heart
Never regards the two apart—
Needful all other things above,
If you would follow, you must love.

ZACCHEUS AND BARTIMEUS.

Mark 10—Luke 19.

ALONG the high-way famed of yore
   Of Jericho the Saviour trod,
Works of mercy his mind before,
   Hail'd David's son, while Son of God.

Out from the city numbers going
   Grew to an eager pressing crowd,
Their hearts with joyfulness o'erflowing,
   Their voices full of praises loud.

'David's great Son is passing by.
  'He comes to bless our sinful race,
'Hail him, behold him, every eye,
  'He comes with heavenly power and grace.'

There was among them one well-known,
  The publican Zaccheus—who
Hearing thus of Christ's renown,
  Resolved he would behold Him too.

By nature dwarf'd he could not see
  His sacred form amid the mass,
But struggling forward climbed a tree
  To watch where he was sure to pass.

Jesus a halting-place soon took
  Just where the road was shadowed o'er,
Prepared with gracious eye to look
  Up to the branching sycamore.

Make haste, Zaccheus, and descend,
  Come down and walk Myself beside;
Make haste, for at the journey's end
  I must at thy house abide.

Zaccheus came with grateful heart,
  The Lord's great goodness warmed it through;
With all his sins resolved to part,
  And for Christ's sake, with riches too.

Always a zealous, ardent man,
  And now taught knowledge from above,
No more a selfish publican,
  He was enlarged with truth and love.

Hear him before the Lord declare,
  "Half of my goods I give the poor,"
My rich possessions they shall share;
  And others too I will secure.

"If any man I've ever wronged"
 'The ill-got gains I will not hold,
 'Whatever unto him belonged
  I will at once restore four-fold."

An envious few to murmur dared,
  That Jesus chose a "sinner's" home;
The Lord, regarding not, declared.
  "Salvation to this house has come."

That very day blind Bartimeus,
  Afflicted son of old Timeus,
Sat begging on the same road-side,
  Heard the same tidings as Zaccheus,
And instantly for mercy cried.

Soon as he heard the crowd draw nigh,
  "Mercy, pity, gracious Lord,
Thou Son of David"! was his cry,
  Repeating oft each earnest word.

Those about him were remonstrant,
    Urging him to hold his peace,
But his cry was louder, constant,
    Jesus, in pity, give release.

His prayers were heard—the blind man brought
    Received his sight with no delay
And grateful for the mercy wrought
    Followed Jesus in the way.

Oh that those blind ones, dark as night,
    Not as to nature's "visual ray,"
But as to inward heavenly light,
    Would learn how good it is to pray!

Remember too the blest Zaccheus,
    How he longed the Lord to see,
How Christ everywhere can see us,
    Even in a sycamore tree.

Zeal to know fully and to taste
   His comforts deeply by His side,
Will bring the welcome words, "make haste,
   To-day I will with thee abide."

Sweet for all time these twain reports
   Of the Lord's goodness on that day—
Long as to Him the heart resorts
   Their memory will not fade away.

BETHANY.

John xi., 25, 26, 27,

TIME was when Bethany was blest
    Beyond most spots which time endears;
Jesus made it His place of rest,
    And hallowed it with love and tears;
And there the proof transcendent gave
Of power divine at Lazarus' grave.
Martha, Mary, and their Brother,
More perhaps than any other,
Impress their histories on the mind,
So rich with sweetest memories twined.

Time was when with intent profound,
Wisdom and love together bound,
He tarried long, and far away
From loved-ones left at Bethany;
Delay still followed by delay.
Meanwhile alarms their bosoms fill,
Their brother Lazarus falls ill.
"He is sick whom thou lovest, Lord"—
Message most touching, pressing word.
But though anxiously, quickly sent,
Nothing but confidence was meant.
No shade of doubtfulness could dim
Their vision of beholding Him
Immediately prepared to come
With love and healing to their home—
Of seeing, should they outward go
To watch the road from Jericho,
His foot-steps, (ah! how far from slow!)
Draw near and nearer to their woe.
They went and gazed with many a tear
For Jesus still did not appear.

He came not—Lazarus grew worse—
He died—he was a buried corse.
Oh! sad mystery, how explain?
With breaking hearts they sought in vain.
At last quick tidings reach them—He
Was on the way described to be.
Martha on the instant rushed
To meet Him, while the fresh tears gushed;
And with a sigh—such rarely sighed!
"Lord, if thou hadst been here," she cried,
"My brother Lazarus had not died."
Mary o'erwhelmed in thought sat still
In sorrow's silent chamber till
Jesus sent for her; then she came
Quickly, sighing forth the same
As Martha, words which notice claim
As showing how intense the thought
Which four days' woe in both had wrought.
But Mary fell down at His feet;
There from affliction her retreat;
Where oft she'd had instruction sweet,
And where she knew was comfort meet.

Now hearken to the wondrous word
Which the astonished sisters heard—
" Thy Brother shall rise again ! "
Said Martha, " Yes, as other men ;
I know that at the Resurrection
He shall arise to life's perfection."
" I am the Resurrection—I
Am the Life—He shall never die
Who Me believes in ; and this word
Believest *thou* ?" she said, " Yea, Lord ! "
Here was the mystery explained,
Here was a glorious knowledge gained ;
Her Brother was to rise e'en *now*,
Jesus the grave would disavow.
He had permitted him to die,
Doubtless without death's agony ;
And his loved spirit passed away
Gently, brief time apart to stay.
The Lord's true purpose in delay
Till after the eventful day
Was now so clear, a solemn calm
On the poor Sisters dropt as balm ;

And we are not to think His love
Wanting in tenderness to prove
It's full perfection—sad was He
To see the fatal malady,
And the helpless sorrowers' need
Vainly requiring urgent speed.
But 'twas His great and gracious will
His faithful ones with joy to fill,
Exhibiting a marvel,—one
The most stupendous He had done;
Honouring His Father's power
By the grand witness of that hour—
Witness the whole world to convince
He was Himself of Life the Prince.

All were assembled bowed with woe;
Hope spread, but nature made it so.
Jesus beheld them weeping, and
Friends alike mourning close at hand,
Who from Jerusalem were there
The visit to the grave to share.

But *who* most deeply touched with grief,
"Groaning in spirit" for relief?
"Where have ye laid him?" "Come, Lord, see,"
The sisters led Him tremblingly.
How softly, silently they stept!
Jesus, Chief-mourner, with them "wept."
"Lazarus! come forth!"—forth he came,
Instantly rising to his name.
Jesus cried, "Loose him, let him go!"
And love, bliss, gladness, banished woe.

And who can doubt, though Holy writ
In simple grandeur doth omit,
That mutual embraces fond,
And joy all utterance beyond
For blessèd Lazarus restored,
Showed how deep was struck the chord
Of gratitude to Christ their Lord.

EASTER DAY.

"He is risen; He is not here; Behold the place where they laid Him."—Mark, 16—6.

OF Holy Days in every year
    Easter is one for ever dear,
In memory of the ruptured tomb,
Pledge of pale death's eternal doom;
Of Angels beautiful and bright,
Instant from the heavenly light,
Administ'ring with love and power
The plans of that eventful hour,
When Jesus, Conqueror in the strife,
Rose from the dead the Prince of Life.

EASTER DAY.

Oh! deeply ponder o'er that grave
Which pious Joseph humbly gave,
And laid upon its rock-hewn bed
In linen fine the treasured dead,
With napkin round the sacred head;
And roll'd a ponderous stone before
The solemn, mournful cavern door.
There shut in darkness cold he lay
Just till the dawn of the Third day,
When at the very moment due
An angel down from heaven flew,
Roll'd back the stone and sat thereon.
His countenance like lightning shone.
And where the Crucified? He's gone,
Risen from out his rocky bed
The "First Begotten from the dead"!

The sepulchre all empty stands,
Save that by some mysterious hands
The relics of the burial bear
Mark'd singularity of care—

The linen clothes together rolled,
The napkin by itself, we're told,
Some truth, it may be, to unfold.

Go to Jerusalem in mind,
In visions of the soul, to find
The glorious truthfulness of all
The wondrous facts blest saints recall,
Eye-witnesses to other ages,
Described in their inspired pages—
Words ever wonderful and new,
And so simple, because true.

Go then to Sion's hallowed hill;
Ponder on scenes all hearts to fill,
Ere superstition marr'd the whole,
And fables through the precincts stole.
First meet upon the crowded way
The crag of doleful Golgotha;
Thence, near at hand, the Saviour's tomb,
Dimly discerned amid the gloom
Of twilight struggling into day.

'Twas there an earthquake burst around,
And frighten'd keepers fled the ground;
'Twas there that hurrying to and fro,
Intent the mystery to know,
Perplexed, distracted, sore-amazed,
Fond weeping women trembling gazed.
They saw the great and heavy stone,
So lately dreaded, overthrown.
They saw the open grave, and bold
Entered—ah! quickly to be told
Him whom they sought it did not hold.
They'd seen Him from the cross conveyed,
And in the tomb of Joseph laid;
They've now brought spices for anointing,
Yet all is sad and disappointing.
But angels there sweet comfort speak—
Jesus is risen whom ye seek;
Dry these now unneeded tears,
Banish doubtfulness and fears;
Just now He issued from the grave
To meet you soon, to bless and save.

Quickly to his disciples go
And tell them all you've seen and know;
And as they went, all joyful, lo!
Jesus was on the way to meet them,
And with the words "All Hail" to greet them.
Falling before His sacred feet,
They clung to them as worship's seat,

These holy women, great their claims
To admiration, and their names
Ever should honoured be—Joanna,
Salome, Mary, and Susanna;
This Mary often called the mother
Of James the Less and of his brother;
Mary of Cleophas the spouse,
A sister in the Virgin's house;
Magdalen, one of Maries three—
Long minist'ring their substance free,
And following Him from Galilee.
Oh! sweet it is so well to know
How many *now* whose bosoms glow

With full devotedness of love
To Him invisible above,
In human needs when Jesus came
Would thankfully have done the same.

MAGDALEN.

MORE PARTICULARLY TRACED.

But Magdalen must ever seem
To shine with a peculiar beam.
See her at first beside the cave
To be her Master's hurried grave;
With anxious Joseph and his friend;
See her devoutly o'er Him bend
The brief embalming to attend;
Watching with the tenderest care,
And eagerly observant where
And how the body was disposed
Ere by the great stone enclosed.

Still, less was done than was required,
Oh! how much less than love desired.
Resolving, then, what would be meet,
To bring with others spices sweet,
The due anointing to complete—
She left—because the Sabbath day
Directed her her homeward way.

"Early the first day of the week"
Again she comes to weep and seek.
The stone gone, there appears to her
No Jesus in the sepulchre.
She'd left His body safely there,
And now the place she knows not where.
Angels instruct, yet broken-hearted
She mourns for Him, the lost, departed;
Seeming in her bewildered mind
To think the body she might find.
To gaze and search she vainly tries,
Darkness with the dawn still vies;
But turning, in the dimness spies

EASTER DAY.

A stranger—instantly she cries,
"If thou hast borne Him hence declare,
"And oh! in pity tell me where;
"Those who love will not forsake Him,
"I will come myself and take Him."
A moment's pause—then in low tone,
The sweetest of a voice well known,
   "MARY"!
And then an earnest, grave reply,
The heart relieved by a deep sigh,
   "RABBONI"!
And this two-worded colloquy
In heart-expressiveness was worth
Thousands of colloquies on earth.

And who this Mary, chief of three?
Once devils held long tenancy—
Jesus Rabboni set her free.

If devils haunt a guilty soul,
And keep it under base control,
Pray to the Lord, in mercy great,

To pity your dejected state;
To drive, to cast them out—and then
Devoted be like Magdalen.

The evening of the day, the same,
An anxious band in secret came
An inner chamber safe to close
Against their bitter Jewish foes.
In converse on the marvels past
Perplexity could not long last;
Soon hope's encouragement grew bright,
And joy increased with further light;
For Magdalen has seen the Lord,
And others have confirmed her word;
Simon, since, above the rest
Of Apostles has been so blest;
Two from Emmaus just returned,
While still their hearts within them burned,
Avouched Him risen from the dead,
And known to them in breaking bread.
Nor to give comfort these alone—

Jesus Himself, their Lord, their Own—
When every door was shut around,
Without a notice or a sound—
Stood in the midst, and saying, "Peace,
"Peace be unto you," gave release
From all their sorrows, while "He showed
His hands and side" from which it flowed.

Oh! would ye penitential be?
Would ye from guilt and sin be free!
Would ye the Saviour's glory see?
Let meditative thoughts abide
On His pierc'd feet, His hands and side.

ASCENSION DAY.

Luke 24, 50—53.   Acts 1, 9—11.

HE leads them forth—His loved and true—
   With them on Olivet he stands,
The well-known Bethany in view,
   And blesses with uplifted hands.

While those raised hands all power possessing,
   Show that they ne'er shall be forsaken,
While those sweet words their hearts addressing
   Are passing from Him—He is "taken."

ASCENSION DAY.

Instantly from their midst ascending
   (Earth cannot hold his heavenward feet)
Higher, higher, higher, till blending
   With glory's cloud sent down to greet.

All strain with rapturous devotion
   To penetrate the mystic veil,
With sorrow's, joy's, and love's emotion
   Gazing, though mortal sight must fail.

Lo! suddenly stand by two men
   In garments of celestial glow,
Who tell them He shall come again
   Just as they now have seen Him go.

Quickly they left the sacred hill,
   And with what joy exultant trod
The Temple courts, continuing still
   In serving, praising, blessing God.

Choice witnesses of Jesu's glory,
   From them we know His heavenly reign;
From them we learn His wondrous story,
   And that He soon will come again.

Believers in his power above
   Within the "everlasting gates!"
Be sure your Lord with faithful love
   The glorious opening hour awaits.

Ye faithful ones oppressed with sadness!
   Ye pilgrims in a world of grief!
The scene on Olivet gives gladness,
   The Blessing there brings full relief.

THE FIRST RESURRECTION.

"THE DEAD IN CHRIST SHALL RISE FIRST."

A CHEERING truth, the sainted dead
   On the great final Easter day,
All quickened from the silent bed
   Shall rising lead the blissful way.

Soon will the far-spent night be ended,
   Soon will the Lord of Glory come,
By holy myriads attended,
   To call His sleepers from the tomb.

'Twill be—however long their slumbers,
    And still in silence they may lie;
And howsoever vast their numbers
    Which have not met Him in the sky;

These now in Jesus sleeping rest,
    Without one missing, one mistaken,
And at the mighty, grand behest,
    The trump of God, will all awaken.

Although their relics widely mingle
    In stony cells, or kindred earth,
Omnipotence at once will single
    Each for a new, immortal birth.

No monuments will then be needed
    To mark and tell each sacred spot;
Nor need the grassy mounds be heeded
    Lest poorer saints should be forgot.

"Them that are His" the Lord well knows,
　　Nor death, nor dust, nor darkness ever,
What time they may mid these repose,
　　Shall from the love of Jesus sever.

Of love how beautiful the token,
　　That for the saints on earth that day
No preference shall be shown or spoken
　　O'er dear ones long since passed away.

Christ's living servants, rapturous all,
　　Must not His dead anticipate;
Though equally belov'd, they shall
　　Their own most wondrous change await.

This marvel wrought—with love unbounded
　　Gathering with His arm of might;
When the last echoing trump is sounded
　　Both shall be rapt to glory's height.

MIDNIGHT TRAVELS.

THE busy world are all for day,
  Sun-light they need in every way;
Night seems for gaiety and slumber,
In each division a vast number.

What would these various parties think
Of midnight hours without a wink
Of sleep, soft comfort, in a bed
Where malady has laid the head?*

* Referring to the fact that these lines, and the larger portion of the sacred pieces in this little book, were written (mentally) at night in a bed of infirmity during the Author's 81st year.

MIDNIGHT TRAVELS.

What would they think, if they could know
How happily such hours flow,
When the heart can fully rest
On thoughts which make affliction blest?

Oft travelling in trance the mind
Delights some sacred scene to find
Immediate, while the body's frame
For feebleness may pity claim.

Yes—and in truth the wakeful hours
Are those wherein the spirit's powers
Are frequently best strung for flight
In earnest watchings of the night.

Rails, telegraphs, electric wires,
Much expedite what man requires;
But for rapidity they're nought
Compared with flashes of bold thought.

I've travelled thus to Bethlehem,
Also to dear Jerusalem
And Olivet, and from the whole
Got deep refreshment for the soul.

Not long since it was Christmas Eve,
Sweet season we with joy receive;
And pondering when the hour came
Entranced I rushed to Bethlehem.

Instantly there—the sheepfolds found—
Glory was shining all around;
Thousands of Angels filled the air
In heavenly melody to share—

All commissioned from above
To join in glorious songs of love—
" Glory to God, to men good will "
For ever and for ever still.

With shepherds to know all intent
Softly and silently I went;
Entering the sacred cave with awe,
Mary, Joseph, the Babe, we saw—

Jesus, Son of the Most High,
In a rude manger seen to lie,
Mary close by Him, Joseph nigh—
These were the Holy Family.

All about Jesus each sweet word
Of Mary and the Shepherds stirred
My listening spirit—and I woke
From a fond dream of what they spoke.

CHRISTMAS 1875.

ONCE again dear Christmas comes
　　To warm our hearts this wintry weather,
To make unnumbered happy homes,
　　And loving ones to bring together.

Parents, children, friends, who may
　　Of late been needfully apart,
On re-uniting Christmas Day
　　Find they've been always near in heart.

It is a blissful, sacred season
　　To meet beside the well-known hearth,
All remembering well the reason
　　For their Saviour's lowly birth.

Thousands of angels from God's throne
    Proclaimed his birth at Bethlehem
In strains of high, seraphic tone,
    Though Jesus was not born for them.

Angels were holy, happy, needing
    Not for themselves salvation, when
With deep delight God's message heeding
    They sang of His "good-will to men."

It was for us, our sinful race,
    That He was born in Bethlehem's cave—
Oh! wonderful, so rude the place
    Where first He dwelt, a world to save.

Of these great truths the recollection
    Must always cling to Christmas Day,
Although it seems the warm affection
    Will needs an earthly form display.

We like the festive preparations
   Welcome guests to please and cheer,
And the warm congratulations
   On the blessed time of year.

We like to see dear faces shining
   In the yule-log's genial glow,
And evergreens with holly twining,
   Nor least, the pendent misletoe.

To young and old 'tis pure delight
   To smile beneath that mirthful bough;
The young, because their eyes are bright,
   The old—'twas once so, though not now.

And if with smiles press'd lips there be,
   (For custom oft will rule it so)
Kind sympathies we well may see
   Spring up beneath the misletoe.

'Tis pleasant still to think upon,
    And good old customs yet to praise;
To know as this our world goes on,
    These were our honoured fathers' ways.

But while hearts o'erflow with gladness,
    And spirits blithe have fullest play,
While converse sweet dispels all sadness,—
    Fórget not 'tis a sacred day.

THE WELL AT BETHLEHEM.

See 2nd Book of Samuel 23, 13—17, compared with 5, 17—8.

Midst a few chosen chiefs to Adullam's steep hold,
Near the pastures where once he conducted his fold,
Judah's minstrel and monarch with weariness came,
And with sadness look'd down o'er the vale of Rephaim.

Proud tents of Philistines far stretched lay below;
In the noon-tide's hot glare shone the spears of the foe;
On the hill-side, beyond the fierce infidel host,
Stood his own native Bethlehem, their fortress and boast.

How oft in that valley and round that fair hill
A young simple shepherd he wander'd at will!
His brow had grown royal with jewels and gold,
Yet the home of his fathers was dear as of old.

Parch'd and faint, his soul long'd for the well-spring
    so clear,
And to reach the loved "gate" he remember'd it near,
Where at morn and at eve he had gather'd his sheep
And drank of its treasures o'erflowing and deep.

Oh! would that I tasted that water once more
From the rock ever gushing, a cool, limpid store!
What hand a fresh cup from that fountain will bring
Which, once free to the shepherd, is barr'd to the king?

Three chieftains beside him drew swords as he spoke;
Down with lion-like hearts on the pagans they broke;
They smote their way through, daring death, to the
    spring,
And fill'd a deep flagon for David their king.

The vessel was brought, but he drank not the wave;
"This water," he cried, "is the blood of the brave;
"And since Heaven has thus honour'd our swords o'er
    the foe
"To none but our God shall it gratefully flow.

"Far, far from the heart of your king be the thought
"To enjoy what the blood of his champions has
    bought."
Then with hand raised on high a libation he poured
Unto Him whom the armies of Israel adored.

HOW SHALL I BE SATISFIED.

ON my pilgrimage below
    Hungering, thirsting, as I go
Through the desert far and wide,
How shall I be satisfied?

Wells and fountains are in vain,
Soon my lips are parch'd again;
"Meat that perisheth" I've tried,
But it never satisfied.

Jesus! I would quench my thirst
Where the "living waters" burst;
If I drink that heavenly tide
I shall then be satisfied.

Let my fainting soul be fed
With the "true" the "living bread;"
With this blessed food supplied
None can be unsatisfied.

Ragged and defiled my dress,
Clothe me in Thy righteousness—
Lamb of God! my vileness hide,
Then will God be satisfied.

Sin indwelling day by day
Makes me mourn upon my way;
Yet, blest Saviour, Thou hast died,
And for sin hast satisfied.

Lead and help me, Lord, to press
Onwards unto holiness;
With the world, with sin and pride,
More and more dis-satisfied.

And when this poor life is o'er,
Shall I thirst or hunger more?
No—for by Immanuel's side
Sinners saved are satisfied.

Then His likeness I shall know,
Then His love will overflow,
And in that eternal tide,
My soul thou shalt be satisfied.*

* "*I shall be satisfied*, when I awake with Thy likeness."—Psalm, 17.15

VERILY I SAY.

BLEST statements in each gospel page,
  Promises which your hearts engage—
Deem all of them prefixed to be
By "Verily I say to thee."

The very chief of sinners *may*
Turn and live, and live for aye.
Here the "Verily" of the Lord
Belongs in truth to every word.

Whosoever comes to me
(No exception shall there be)
I will in no wise cast away,
No, never, "verily I say."

Oh! come in penitence for sin,
Pardoned, the godly life begin;
Come at once, dispel delay,
Come freely, " verily I say."

Ye weary ones, with grief and toil,
With the world's converse and turmoil;
Ye heavy-laden, sore-distressed,
"Come, and I will give you rest."

Perfect peace I give to those
Who on my love their trust repose;
The world may give and take away,
I change not, "verily I say."

And soon will come the final hour
Conclusive of His love and power,
When Jesus, near you, will in Spirit
Tell of the bliss you shall inherit.

VERILY I SAY.

Turn in the true recording Book
To the passage in St. Luke,
Where the same words our thoughts employ
Himself prefixed to promised joy.

The sufferer on the cross beside Him,
E'en while he heard all round deride Him,
Cried, Lord of heaven "remember me,"
When in Thy kingdom Thou shall be!

Oh! ye who love, His answer see—
"*Verily I say to thee,*
This very day thy soul shall be
Safe in paradise with me."

STANDING AND KNOCKING.

'TIS JESUS knocking at the door—
    Does not the inmate hear the sound?
Does slumber steep his senses o'er?
    Or *indifferent* is he found?
How awful thus to treat His Name,
Careless to be of whence He came!

Still the great Visitant stands there,
    His hand yet patiently in place
Upon the knocker—oh! beware
    Of slighting such transcendent grace.

All the way from heaven He's come
To tell about a loftier home;
And until there His faithful go,
To dwell among them here below.

To be a guest within the heart
The sweetest comforts to impart.
He says, " I will come in, and he
"Shall sup in mutual love with Me."

Those happy ones who heard His knock,
   And hearing hastened to undo
The stubborn bar, the stiffened lock,
   Were earnest and successful too.
He entered at their open door,
And they are blest for evermore.

Alas! the evil case of those
   Whose hearts are hardened, shut up fast;
These are the doors that wont unclose,
   And seem determined to the last.

STANDING AND KNOCKING.

From an opening casement near
Does a disturbed, quick eye appear?
Observing Him who stands before
Holding the knocker at the door,

Him above all that e'er are seen
For goodness, grace, and lovely mien?
Yet does a voice assault His ear,
"Go—there is no admittance here?,'

Or is no voice, no notice heard?
Is there not said a single word?
No,—but a hand is quickly passed
To pull the lattice close and fast.

What before all should most be prized
Is thus rejected and despised.
How mournful such hard hearts to see,
And oh! how patient Christ must be!

List'ning—list'ning even yet—
His tender ear intently set,
If haply there should on it fall
A footstep—but 'tis silence all.

How can He longer list'ning stand?
Must not the knocker lose His hand?
Must He not mournful leave the door
To turn again—ah! nevermore?

But oh! this thought a moment check,
This dreadful thought of utter wreck.
Should there be one misgiving felt,
One token that the heart may melt,

Thou, Lord, the faintest sign can'st see,
From hardness, hindrance, thou cans't free,
Near or far off the same may be—
"For all is possible with Thee."

HARVEST HOME.

"So shall it be in the end of this world-"
Mat. 13—30.

SEE, the sickle's work is ending,
    Yellow sheaves in piles appear;
Reapers binding, teams attending,
    Soon the burdened field will clear.

—So when "time shall be no longer,"
    Angels the wide world will reap;
Flaming swords than lightning stronger
    All in one vast host shall sweep.

In the spacious barn are lifted
    Thousand shocks, a towering store;
There their value must be sifted
    On the Master's threshing-floor.

—Comes that day, great day of wonder,
    All before their Judge shall stand,
Till a voice more dread than thunder
    Summon them on either hand.

When the heavy flail resoundeth,
    When the winnowing fan's in play,
How each worthless grain reboundeth,
    How the light chaff whirls away!

—Thus the vain, the vile, shall vanish,
    Driven to darkness, grief and shame;
Christ from heaven and bliss will banish
    Those whose deeds denied His name.

But the true, the solid treasure,
　　Still remains in shining heaps ;
This the Master views with pleasure
　　And within His garner keeps.

—They who "love their Lord's appearing"
　　Thus shall meet His beaming face,
And amidst angelic cheering
　　Find with Him their resting-place.

DAVID'S HARP.

WITH harp in hand young David came
    His sovereign's troubled soul to tame.
In shepherd-guise before him brought,
He touched the chords with pious thought;
The strain to Israel's God addressed
Dispell'd the fiend and charmed to rest.

When David owned that monarch's throne
His harp was still for God alone:
He knew who "took him from the fold,"
And bound his youthful brow with gold,
And, as he played, the grateful strings
Rang praises to the King of Kings.

DAVID'S HARP.

With psalteries shrill and trumpets loud,
With priests and chiefs, a joyful crowd,
He bore unto a holier place
The ark of covenanted grace;
While, as the sacred train advanced
He swept his echoing harp and danced.

At morn his harp was ever strung,
For then a hymn of praise he sung;
And ever at the close of day
His harp led on the thankful lay;
For every note of every chord
He consecrated to the Lord.

FROM THE GERMAN.

NOT to be too elate in blissful days,
Nor to be crush'd when grief its burden lays;
To bear, in life's routine, what needs must be,
The unavoidable, with dignity;
To act as conscience dictates to be right;
In all that's excellent to take delight;
To love and to enjoy existence here,
Yet death's conclusive summons not to fear;
Firmly in God a pious faith to hold
For what the better future shall unfold—
Thus living is to give to life success,
And death deprive of all its bitterness.

YOUNG EDWARD'S GRAVE.

SEASONS have past, my Loved One, since we laid
   Thy gentle form beneath that sacred sward,
Few days without a silent visit paid
To muse in anguish upon Heaven's award,
Doubtless most wise, tho' seemingly so hard;
Few days that witness'd not a tender care
From heedless feet the treasured space to guard,
And nurse some simple flowers to scent the air,
Emblems of Thee, who once, like them, wast sweet
   and fair,

Young yews and cypresses stood mourning round,
And sapling willows waved and wept above,
And sweet-briars closely fenced the narrow mound
With poignant wreaths that breathed of aching love;

And o'er the old brown wall a bordering grove
Of loftier boughs did broader shadows throw,
Where, guiltless of offence, were wont to rove
Songsters unconscious all of human woe,
Or nestle o'er their young while mine slept cold below.

And near was many a varied-figured stone,
All tokens of the love which placed them there;
Some moss'd by years gone by, where children lone
Came in the stillness of sweet evening's air
To mourn, thought-stricken, lost parental care;
Some fresh, to mark, alas! where young ones lay,
Their home's warm bosom never more to share;
But cherish'd still, like mine, by night and day
Within the broken heart, till hearts are all decay.

Ah! when the well-known bell in yonder tower
Tolls forth in monotones its heavy sounds,
And all confess its melancholy power;

And in the midst of scatter'd grassy mounds
Turfless appears in short and narrow bounds
A youthful grave ; and weepers slowly come
To close it—opening all the bosom's wounds ;
The heart must needs recall an earlier tomb,
So like this sadden'd scene, this unexpected doom.

My child ! my loved and lovely one, 'twas long
Ere grief could more than muse beside that spot,
And memory utter e'en a plaintive song ;
Yet Heaven, in mercy, whisper'd of thy lot
Where bliss unites with life, and endeth not :
And now, more deeply heard, those whispers fall
To soothe for that which ne'er can be forgot ;
To bid me, in life's ills and perils, call
Ever the thought to rise that Thou art safe from all.

A MEDITATION.

OUR days are in the "sere and yellow leaf"—
    And winter's sweeping wind comes moaning by,
Can nature be susceptible of grief?
    Or is the moaning wind a conscious sigh?
Nature itself is destitute of mind,
Cause and effect alone are intertwined
By Him, the All-wise One, who all designed,
And by omnipotence the whole combined.
'Tis only man of creatures here below
Can what he sees intelligently know,
Can in the marvels every where around
Read lessons for himself which there abound,
Can thus in woodland scenes and forest glades,

A MEDITATION.

Where in autumnal days the foliage fades,
Mark the leaves "sere and yellow" in decay
Fluttering with feeble hold upon the spray
Till winter comes and scatters them away.
How solemnly the words of Holy Writ,
And closely too, our circumstances fit!
" *We* all do fade as leaves" when comes their day,
Which "the wind" severs from their native stay;
But 'tis our sins that " take *ourselves* away."*
Ponder the awful truth these words convey.
Oh! may those sins be cancelled, and their power
Destroyed before the look'd-for final hour!
May He, the Merciful in might and will,
Say to the raging tempest, " Peace, be still."
May comfort of the perfect "calm" be known,
And thankfulness be felt for mercies shown!
And oh! at last, may one deep sense of grief
Through soothings of sweet hopes have some relief,
Small though it must be, for fond hearts must grieve
The lov'd, the Dearest ones, behind to leave.

* Isaiah ch. 64—v. 6.

THE OCTOGENARIAN.

THE period Three Score Years and Ten
    Assigned to be the age of men,
Is oft afflicted e'er its close
With weakness, sufferings and woes;
But long before the look'd for time,
In earliest youth, in manhood's prime,
At every age, with fluctuation,
Multitudes past calculation
Die under seventy years—thus then
Those of three-score years and ten
Are a minority of men.
Great numbers seventy reach 'tis true,
(In this we may th' assignment view)
But in comparison they're few.

Four Score years may be attained—
Can it be said that they are *gained ?*
Yes—if such aged ones are found
In truth and goodness to abound;
If their honoured whitened locks
Tell of affliction's many shocks,
Nor less of services to all
Done heartily at duty's call—
But if not so, and unprepared,
Although so long in this world spared,
Now thou art so near life's border,
Old man, "set thy house in order."

Many affecting thoughts belong
To what saith Holy Writ—" So strong
" Men are, they come to four score years,
" Yet is their strength then labour—tears—
" Passing so soon, and they are gone."
Solemn reflection thereupon ·
Is fit and wise ;—and solemn too
As mournful, the old man's review

Of those, the many friends so dear,
Who dropt behind him year by year,
Together journeying life's stages
Till parted by unequal ages,
Leaving him still one by one
Until at last they all are gone,
And with sadness he must own
That now he walks the world alone.
But though on earth with him no more,
He trusts they've reached the peaceful shore
Together talk'd of oft before
As true and precious heavenly lore.

Many a token yet remains
Which he carefully retains,
Proving how genuine and true-hearted
Was the regard of the departed.
Much that gave interest long before
Now comes from recollection's store—
The converse frequent, and so pleasant,

From the kind feelings always present;
Seasons and places where such words
Faithful memory still records;
The winter evenings' fire-side talk,
In summer days the cheering walk,
Excursions in our charming June,
Quiet rambles when the moon
Her silvery light shed o'er the scene
More beautiful than mid-day's sheen.
Yet with all these soothing things
Which gratified remembrance brings,
Wonder not if the old man's tear
Should for a moment re-appear.

Nor is it rare at eighty years,
Methinks, that sometimes silent tears
Still drop for a long parted Child.
Though many years on years are piled,
How can the heart be reconciled?
One well I know, surviving yet
The ills of life that he has met,
Who long since lost one passing dear;

In token of whose memory here
A hair-set ring is treasured near,
And fondest thoughts upon it linger
Placed on a now poor shrivelled finger,
Fitting but loosely, and which may
From trivial causes slip away;
But he'd tell you—"I still will use it—
"Love makes it safe—I shall not lose it."

But there's another state of things
Which other thoughts most fitly brings.
Head of a second generation,
He holds a dfferent relation,
He's a Grandsire, and proudly sees
The little Ones before his knees
In all their loveliness, and bright
With innocence and young delight,
And blissful to him is the sight.
But ah! 'tis nothing he can know
Of what may hap them here below;
He cannot reach beyond the scope

Of ardent wishes, trustful hope;
A glance that charms his loving eye
Sees not into destiny,
Nor even near futurity,
And can he suppress a sigh?
But he can pray— he does— he will—
That our Good God will keep them still
In this bad world from every ill:
That She, his Blest Beloved on earth,
Who so rejoiced him by their birth,
May live to mark their minds unfold
In beauty of the heavenly mould;
At last confiding Her and Them,
Lov'd Offspring of so lov'd a stem,
And Him who owns her as his gem,
To the safe care whate'er befal
Of the Great Father of us all.

www.ingramcontent.com/pod-product-compliance
Lightning Source LLC
Chambersburg PA
CBHW020126170426
43199CB00009B/654